CHARLIE and ALICE

Finding a Friend

Written by Deborah Abela
Illustrated by Stefano Tambellini

Published by Pearson Education Limited, Edinburgh Gate, Harlow, Essex,
CM20 2JE
Registered company number: 872828

www.pearsonschools.co.uk

Original illustrations © Pearson Education Limited, 2012
Illustrated by Stefano Tambellini
Cover design by Bigtop

First published 2012

23
12

British Library Cataloguing in Publication Data
A catalogue record for this book is available from the British Library

ISBN 978 0 435 07593 4

Printed in the UK

Acknowledgements
We would like to thank the children and teachers of Bangor Central
Integrated Primary School, NI; Barley Hill School, Thame; Bishop Henderson
C of E Primary School, Somerset; Brookside Community Primary School,
Somerset; Catcott Primary School, Somerset; Cheddington Combined
School, Buckinghamshire; Cofton Primary School, Birmingham; Dair
House Independent School, Buckinghamshire; Deal Parochial School, Kent;
Lawthorn Primary School, North Ayrshire; Newbold Riverside Primary
School, Rugby and Windmill Primary School, Oxford for their invaluable
help in the development and trialling of the Bug Club resources.

Every effort has been made to contact copyright holders of material
reproduced in this book. Any omissions will be rectified in subsequent
printings if notice is given to the publisher.

Contents

Chapter 1
A Million Miles from Home

Alice sat on the bench of the ferry as the city drifted further behind her. She had a rucksack at her feet and on her lap was a small brown bear. His fur had been rubbed off in places and he had one brown eye and one green one that had been sewn on. Alice

held him tightly in her arms, one finger
rubbing his belly.

The ferry sailed under a grey sky. The
wind was cold and bullying, whipping the
ocean spray into her face. Alice held the bear
up and breathed in his familiar smell.

It reminded her of home. Like she was
still there and everything was back to how it
should be.

"Don't worry, Barney," she whispered.
"I'll look after you."

Alice was far away from home and getting further with each passing wave. Home had felt far away from the moment she'd been called into the headteacher's office and everything was made to look different. Now it felt as if she was living someone else's life, where nothing was familiar and where she didn't belong.

Chapter 2
In the Headteacher's Office

Alice looked up when she heard her name being called.

"Alice White?" The office lady stood at the door. "You need to bring all your belongings and come with me."

Everyone turned and stared, wondering why Alice had been called. She was wondering the same thing herself.

She walked through the maze of desks and down the corridor. The office lady, who had never really noticed her before, gave her the look she gave other children when they were really ill. Alice smiled to let her know she was fine, but it only made the office lady's look even worse.

Alice heard voices and somebody crying. She felt as if she was intruding and should go back to class, but the office lady's hand was on her shoulder, directing her towards the crying. It was then that Alice realised who it was. She tried to take a deep breath, but felt as if her chest had been squeezed of air.

"In you go, sweetheart."

Alice opened the door to see her mum slumped in a chair, dabbing her nose with a hanky. She instantly sat up, put on a smile and wiped her eyes. Her hair was a mess, which was something Alice's mother would normally never let happen.

"Your brother is ill again and we've had to take him to hospital," her mum said. "Everything is going to be fine, but for now you're going to stay with Grandma."

"What about school?"

"The holidays begin in two days," the headteacher smiled. "You can start them early."

Alice's mum stood up. "Your bag's packed and there's a taxi waiting outside."

So that was it. Alice was bundled into the car by her mum, who paid the driver.

She put on her seat belt and turned to
wave goodbye, but her mum was already
walking away.

Chapter 3
Arriving at Grandma's

Alice's cold hand gripped the railing as she made her way off the ferry. Grandma was on the dock, looking as if she'd been waiting for hours. Alice held Barney and stared at the old wooden ferry terminal that she had been coming to for years. The same wide windows looking out to sea, the same smoke coiling up from its crooked chimney, but somehow, it felt unfamiliar.

Her grandma swooped in with one of her usual warm and cuddly hugs, but even that felt different.

"You've brought Barney." Grandma ruffled the scruffy teddy. "I haven't seen him for a long time."

Alice hugged Barney even closer.

"Well, it's good to see both of you. I bet you're famished. I've got a feast fit for a princess *and* her bear," she smiled.

Alice had never been here on her own before. She'd always arrived with her family or her brother, Simon. Now it was just her. Apart from Barney, of course.

Chapter 4
The First Few Days

For the first few days, Alice only wanted to smother herself in blankets until she got the call to go home. Lying in bed, she would sometimes wake to hear Grandma talking in the kitchen. Alice would race down the stairs two at a time, only to see Grandma hang up the phone.

"Was that Mum?"

"Yes, dear, she rang to make sure we're okay."

"Did she want to say hello to me?"

"Of course she did, but they're very busy. She sends you her love and told me to do this." Grandma gave Alice a kiss on each cheek. "Now I hope you're hungry because there's a stack of blueberry pancakes coming right up."

Alice wasn't hungry. In fact, she couldn't imagine eating anything ever again. She felt as if moving away from her family had sucked the flavour out of her world and left it tasting bland and hopeless.

Alice plonked herself down on a chair. "Why don't my parents want me?"

Grandma stopped stirring the pancake batter and sat beside her. "Your parents adore you. They couldn't love you any more because that would be impossible."

Alice began to cry. "Then why did they send me away?"

Grandma's arms were warm around her. "So you wouldn't worry about your brother. That's a job for the grown-ups."

"But I'm not that young any more."

"As soon as there's news, they'll call, but right now there isn't much anyone can do but wait."

Chapter 5
A Bad Dream

Alice stepped closer to the hospital bed
where Simon lay, hardly breathing. She
lifted her hand to feel his forehead. When
she did, the beeping machine beside him
stopped. Doctors raced into the room and
Alice's parents rushed in behind them
shouting, "What have you done?"

Alice's heart froze. "Nothing, I just wanted to …"

"We told you to stay away," her father said.

The doctors fussed around her brother.

Alice stood back. "Please be okay," she whispered. "Please, please …"

Alice sat up and gulped air into her dry throat. Her chest heaved and her hair was plastered to her forehead with sweat.

Her grandmother rushed in, threw open the curtains and nestled in beside her.

"Alice, I'm here. What's wrong?"

"Is Simon okay?"

"No change yet. Did you have a bad dream? You were crying out."

Alice calmed down a little. "Can we call them?"

"They aren't allowed to have their mobile phones on in the hospital, sweetie."

Alice closed her eyes and tried to wipe away the last of the nightmare.

Her grandma snuggled her in for a hug. "Everything's going to be fine. You'll see. I'll be downstairs making breakfast. Fresh strawberries and home-made yogurt this morning. Come down when you're ready."

Alice stared at the crumpled mess of blankets around her. She sighed and looked out of the window. There were blue skies and green hills rolling down to the sea. In the past she would have jumped out of bed and raced downstairs for a big breakfast before spending the day exploring.

Today she just wanted to curl into bed and shut herself away. Then she saw a boy standing on a hill nearby, looking through a telescope into the distance. She poked her head out of the window for a better view.

At that exact moment, he stood back from the telescope and turned directly towards her. He smiled and waved. Alice quickly ducked inside, hoping she hadn't been seen, but when she stole another look, he waved again.

Alice grabbed hold of the curtains and pulled them closed. Then she slipped under the blankets, wishing the whole world would leave her alone.

Chapter 6
Meeting Charlie

Alice was eating her breakfast when the boy arrived at the door of the kitchen. He was all arms and legs and had a fringe that fell in his face.

"I wondered when you might visit," Grandma said. "Have you had breakfast?"

"Yep. Two helpings."

"Alice, this is Charlie Fisher from next door."

Alice gave a small nod.

"I was wondering if you wanted to have a go with my telescope," Charlie smiled. "You get a great view across the bay from Mays Hill."

"Thanks," Alice said. "But I don't feel well, so I'm going to stay here."

Charlie's smiled slipped a little. "Maybe another time."

"That's a good idea, Charlie." Grandma's hand rested on his shoulder. "Maybe another time."

Chapter 7
Cartwheels and Handstands

The next morning, Alice raced downstairs when her grandma called her name.

"It's your mum." She handed Alice the phone.

"Mum? Yes, yes I'm fine. No, it's been okay, but when can I …"

Alice listened, her smile slowly fading. "Okay, but I just want to know when …"

Alice gave the phone back. "She had to go."

Grandma kissed her on the head and nodded towards the window. "He's here again."

Alice sneaked a quick look. Charlie was outside doing cartwheels and walking on his hands.

"I think you two would like each other."

"I have friends at home."

"Oh, but you can never have too many friends."

There was a knock on the door. Alice shot her grandma a pleading look and ran upstairs. She hid behind her bedroom door and listened.

"Would Alice like to come exploring?"

"Sorry, Charlie," Grandma said. "She doesn't feel like it today. Maybe tomorrow."

Upstairs, Grandma found Alice in bed. "Charlie's a nice boy. He comes over and helps chop wood, or runs errands for me." She stroked Alice's cheek. "A friend can help you take your mind off things."

"I want to be near the phone for when Mum calls and says I can go home." Alice stopped. "I'm sorry, it's not that I don't want to be with you … it's just …"

"I know." Grandma smiled and softly closed the door.

Alice stared out of the window from behind her curtain. In the distance, Charlie turned and looked straight at her. He smiled and kept walking.

Chapter 8
A Little Accident

Charlie came over every morning for a week. When Alice opened her curtains, he'd be there. She hugged Barney as she watched Charlie juggle, badly, or balance books on his head, adding one more every so often, until they tumbled to the ground in a heap.

Alice laughed and Charlie bowed.

One morning when Alice opened her curtains, Charlie was balancing his bike on its back wheel. He circled the farmyard, twisting and turning … until his front wheel slammed into the ground. He flew off the bike and landed in the soggy mess of the cows' feeding trough.

Alice jumped from her bed and raced downstairs.

"Are you okay?" She tried to help Charlie up. "Are you hurt?"

He wiped some soggy hay from his cheek. "I knew my charm would get you out here soon enough."

Alice put her hands on her hips. "I came out because I thought you were hurt."

"Not because I'm charming?" Charlie pretended to be offended as he took bits of hay out of his hair. "My mum says I'm the most charming person she knows."

"She's your mum, so she's supposed to say that."

"I got you to come outside, though! Do you want to go exploring with me?"

Alice frowned at the mushy foodscraps he still had plastered to him. "Maybe."

"Excellent!" Charlie climbed out of the trough.

"I said, maybe."

"A maybe's better than a no."

Grandma appeared at the door. "Did she give in, Charlie?"

"Yes, my charm *finally* worked."

"Charm?" Alice cried. "He almost killed himself and I had to rescue him."

Grandma winced. "Well, you definitely didn't win her over because of how you look. How about you go home and shower? I'll have a stack of hot pancakes waiting for you when you get back."

Chapter 9
The First Adventure

Charlie wiped the maple syrup from his mouth and grabbed his rucksack. "Ready to explore?"

"Explore?" Grandma smiled at Alice. "What a great idea." She winked at Charlie and packed some fruit and a drink into Alice's bag. "Don't go too far, and be careful of the bull next door. Just keep him at a distance and go through the next field."

Charlie whistled his way into the sunshine and Alice followed.

"You don't give up easily, do you?" Alice asked.

"If I did, you'd be missing out on my dazzling personality."

"Where are you and your dazzling personality taking me?"

"Somewhere special." Charlie flashed Alice a wide smile and they walked in silence for a few moments. "Why are you staying here?"

"My little brother's in hospital and my parents are too busy to take care of me."

"What's wrong with him?"

"They won't say. They keep telling me he has weak lungs but that everything's going to be fine."

"Why don't they just tell you what's wrong?"

"Because they don't want me to worry. Dad says that worrying too much makes you short and I'm short enough already. He thinks he's being funny."

"Dad Syndrome," Charlie shrugged. "As soon as someone becomes a dad, their sense of humour warps so that they aren't actually funny any more."

Alice laughed. "My dad has a bad case of it then. What are your mum and dad like?"

"They're great. They let me do what I want. Mum is the best. She's always singing and laughing. There it is." Charlie pointed to a nearby hill. "Race you to the top!"

He sped off with Alice close behind.

Chapter 10
A View Fit for a Queen and King

Charlie reached the top of the hill first and flopped down on the grass beneath a large oak tree.

"Beat you," he puffed.

"You had a head start."

"That's just an excuse," Charlie smiled. "Welcome to Mays Hill. My favourite place."

Alice tried to catch her breath. "I haven't been up here for years. It's nice."

"Wait until you see this." Charlie took his telescope from his pack and began setting it up.

Alice looked through the viewfinder. Beyond the farmland and bay, she could make out the city with its church spires, rows of huddled houses and castle on the hill.

Charlie pointed. "Down there's your gran's house and my place too."

Alice spotted both homes. "They're so small!"

"The world looks different through a telescope. It's like everything is just there and you can almost reach out and touch it. We can be the king and queen watching over our kingdom, making sure everyone's okay. Is your brother in hospital in the city?"

Alice nodded.

"What's he like?"

"He's the favourite child. He's been ill since he was a baby, so Mum and Dad fuss over him and hardly even remember I'm around." Alice sighed. "He's cute, I guess, and he gives good cuddles."

"I wish I had a little brother," Charlie said. "I'd teach him how to swim and climb trees."

"Not how to be charming?" Alice smiled.

Charlie smiled back. "If he hung out with me, being charming would rub off automatically."

Chapter 11
Visitors in Suits

Alice had been waiting for Charlie to arrive since she'd finished breakfast. They were going exploring again, but he hadn't turned up. As she sat and waited with Barney, she noticed a car in the distance. It stopped outside Charlie's house.

A man and woman dressed in suits went inside and seemed to stay for ages. When they left, Alice waited for Charlie but he didn't come out.

"Come on, Barney, let's go and see what's happening."

Alice climbed over the fence and walked across the fields to Charlie's house. When she knocked, an older woman answered. She had kind eyes and wisps of grey hair swept into a bun.

"I'm Alice, a friend of Charlie's. He was going to come over."

"Alice, we've been hearing so much about you." The woman's smile fell a little. "Charlie's had bad news from home."

Alice was confused. "But isn't *this* his home?"

"We try to make it feel that way, but this is Charlie's foster home."

"But he said ..." Alice stopped. "Why doesn't he live with his real mum and dad?"

"I'm sorry, love. It's up to Charlie if he wants to tell you that." She brushed a strand of hair out of Alice's eyes. "We love Charlie. He seems to like living here, and since he met you, he's been even happier."

"Can I see him?"

"Of course you can." The woman led the way up the stairs and knocked on a door before entering, but Charlie was gone.

"Charlie?" She checked a few more rooms. "He's never gone out before without telling me."

Alice thought for a moment. "I know exactly where he'll be."

Chapter 12
Finding Charlie Fisher

Alice let the door slam behind her and raced down the path. She tore across the mounds of grass and climbed over a fence into an open field. When she got to the top of Mays Hill, she saw Charlie with his knees bunched up to his chest, staring across the bay.

Alice walked slowly towards him and sat
down. "You were supposed to come over."

"I'm sorry." Charlie's usual smile was
missing. He dug a fingernail into his
thumb. "I got this splinter and I can't seem
to get it out. Normally they don't bother me
but this one really hurts."

His eyes were red and swollen and had a frightened look in them that Alice hadn't seen before.

"I know about you being in foster care," she said.

Charlie stopped digging at his thumb.

"Why didn't you tell me?" asked Alice.

Charlie shrugged. "There didn't seem much point when I was going home soon."

"So you'd have left without telling me?"

"No, I wouldn't," Charlie frowned. "It just felt easier pretending for a while that everything was okay." He looked away. "I didn't want you to think I was strange, either."

"I'd never think that."

"You might when you know the truth."

"Trust me." Alice crossed her heart.

Charlie took a big breath. "My mum and I have lived in lots of different places in the city. Just when we'd get settled, we'd have to move, usually because Mum had to hide from people she owed money to. My mum's a good person; she just forgets things and is easily confused. The last time it happened, the social worker decided that if I had some time in foster care, Mum would be able to concentrate on getting herself sorted out."

"What about your dad?"

Charlie's head hung low. "He left when I was a baby." He paused. "Now do you think I'm strange?"

Alice shook her head. "I think you're fine just as you are. What did the people in the suits want?"

Charlie picked at the splinter. "I was supposed to go home next week, but Mum's decided she needs more time." He couldn't stop the tears that had been threatening to fall. "I just want to go home."

Alice took his hand. "You will. For a while, though, you have two places to call home – here, and with your mum, when she's ready."

"She'll be ready. She told me."

"For now, then, it means you're stuck with me, which can't be all that bad."

Charlie smiled.

Alice reached into her pocket. "Here's a tissue. It's clean."

"I miss her," Charlie said quietly.

"I'm sure she misses you too. I know it's not the same as having your mum, but you've got me." Alice's eyes widened. "I bet it'll help if you write her a letter and then you can tell her how you feel."

Charlie shook his head and mumbled, "She knows how I feel."

"But a letter is something she can keep, like you're always with her."

Charlie dug at his splinter again. "I'm not very good at that kind of thing." There were more tears in his eyes. "I haven't been able to get to school very often so I don't write very well. Anyway, I don't have her new address. Only my foster parents know where she lives."

Alice paused before deciding.

"Well, I love writing. Either I can help with the spelling, or you can tell me what to say and I'll write it. Your foster parents can send the letter for you."

"Would you really do that?"

"When I arrived at my grandma's, I was so miserable. All I wanted to do was leave. Then I met you, Charlie Fisher, and all that changed. The least I can do is help you write a letter home. But first, let's go back so everyone can stop worrying."

Alice jumped to her feet and held out
her hand for Charlie. He took it and stood
beside her. "Thank you."

"You're welcome," Alice said. "Now, how
would you like to start that letter?"